Yao Ming

Yao Ming

by John Hareas

SCHOLASTIC INC.
New York   Toronto   London   Auckland   Sydney
Mexico City   New Delhi   Hong Kong   Buenos Aires

To my All-Star readers, Emma and Christopher
—J.H.
Special Thanks: BDA Sports Management: Bill Duffy, Bill Sanders,
Erik Zhang, Jane Yin

Yao Ming, Colin Pine

ISBN 0-439-59108-2

12 11 10 9 8 7 6 5   4 5 6 7 8/0

Printed in the U.S.A.
First Scholastic printing, November 2003
Book Design: Louise Bova

Contents

Meet Yao Ming

Yao Ming is funny. The seven-foot, five-inch center from China loves to make people laugh. Yao loves to laugh, too, even at himself.

"He's a happy guy," said his former Houston Rockets coach Rudy Tomjanovich. "He's got a good outlook on life and he's just fun to be around."

But on the court, Yao is very serious. He is a complete player who can score, grab rebounds and block shots. It helps that he is one of the tallest players in the NBA.

Yao entered the NBA in 2002. He was a big hit, on and off the court. He made almost half his shots, and averaged 13.5 points and 8.2 rebounds per game in his first season. Everywhere he went, cameras followed. Fans from his homeland and around the world watched every Rockets game. Yao got 1,286,324 votes for the 2002 NBA All-Star Game. It was the third-highest vote total!

Everything was new to Yao in his first year in America. Playing in the NBA was different from playing in China. The game is faster in the NBA and features the greatest players in the world. Yao also had to adjust to a new city, a new language

and new foods. To help him, Yao's parents moved from China to Houston. Yao also had an interpreter to help him speak with reporters. Yao spoke Mandarin Chinese, but did not speak English very well. He worked hard to get better. He also learned how to drive a car!

In his free time, Yao likes to use his computer.

He chats with his friends back home and plays computer games. He also likes to learn about American culture. He will have plenty of opportunities. Yao will be a star in the NBA for a long time.

Growing Up

Yao Ming was born on September 12, 1980, in Shanghai, China. He is an only child. Both his mom, Fang Feng Di, and dad, Yao Zhi Yuan, were star basketball players in China. They are tall, just like Yao. Yao's mom is 6-3 and played for China's national team. His dad is 6-10. He played for Shanghai's top professional team.

When Yao was a kid, people in Shanghai expected him to be a star basketball player, just like his parents. Yao's parents did not pressure him to play. But Yao *wanted* to play.

He first started to play basketball at the age of nine. He was enrolled in the Youth Sports School in Shanghai and, at first, Yao wasn't very good at basketball.

"I couldn't shoot at all," said Yao. "I could only make a layup if no one else was around."

Basketball was not the only game Yao liked to play. He enjoyed playing volleyball and Ping-Pong. He had many other hobbies, too.

"I liked making paper airplanes and paper

boats," said Yao. "I also played a lot of video games."

One of the things Yao loved most was riding his bike. "I enjoyed riding my bike to school every day," said Yao. "I remember smelling the delicious aromas from the breakfast stands."

By age 12, Yao was 6-6. He tried playing water polo at a sports academy. But he only played for two months.

"They kicked me off the team because my skill level was too far behind," said Yao. "I couldn't swim fast enough."

Yao did not mind. As he got older, basketball became his focus. At age 14, Yao tried out for the local junior professional team, the Shanghai Sharks. He made the team. It would be the start of something amazing.

A Star on the Rise

Yao was excited to make the Shanghai Sharks junior team. It was a big honor. It also was a lot of hard work. Yao moved out of his

parents' house to train for the team. He was away from home for nearly six months. It was a lot of pressure for a 14-year-old.

"The junior team could pick players from 10 different schools within the district," said Yao. "You would train, and people would get cut. Only the best players would get to the Shanghai team."

Yao was clearly one of the best players.

This is when Yao saw his first NBA game on television. It was Game 1 of the 1994 NBA Finals between the Houston Rockets and New York Knicks. Yao liked what he saw. He watched the rest of those final games — they made a big impression on him. One of the players, Hakeem Olajuwon of the Rockets, soon became one of his all-time favorites.

When he was a child, Yao loved geography and

history. His childhood dream was "to be [an] adventurer and explore the world." Eventually, his basketball career would allow him to live his childhood dream.

When Yao was 17, basketball let him travel to Paris with a national youth team. Yao played well and the basketball scouts started to notice him.

Soon, Yao moved up to the Sharks' senior national team. He averaged 10.2 points and 8.3 rebounds in his first season. Suddenly, he was a star. Everyone wanted to see Yao play.

But Yao wanted to get even better. At age 17, Yao visited the United States for the very first time. He played in an international basketball tournament in San Diego. He also attended Michael Jordan's basketball camp in Santa Barbara, California.

After his trip to the United States, Yao began to dream of playing in the NBA. Each year, he got better and better. His scoring average climbed from 10.2 points to 32.6 points per game! In 2002, he led the Sharks to the Chinese Basketball Association title. Yao was awesome in the CBA Finals. He averaged 41.3 points, 21.0 rebounds and 4.3 blocks against the Bayi Rockets. He was named the CBA Sportsmanship Award winner!

In 2000, Yao played on the Chinese Olympic team.

"That's the pinnacle," said Yao. "I don't think there are any greater games on Earth."

Yao played against the U.S. team that featured NBA All-Stars Tim Duncan, Kevin Garnett and Vince Carter. Even though China lost to the United States, Yao was able to test his skills against the world's best. Two years later, Yao competed against the U.S. team again in the 2002 World Championships.

It was very exciting for Yao to play against some of the best players in the NBA. Things were about to get even more exciting — very soon, Yao would be playing *with* them.

Coming to America

A few years ago, the Houston Rockets was one of the worst teams in the NBA. The Rockets finished the 2001–02 season with a 28–54 record. Then they got lucky. The Rockets got the number one pick in the NBA Draft lottery. The last time the Rockets had the top overall pick was in 1984. Back then, the team chose a skinny

center from the University of Houston. His name? Hakeem Olajuwon. It turned out to be a fantastic pick. Ten years later, Olajuwon led the Rockets to back-to-back NBA titles.

In 2002, the Rockets already had an All-Star guard in Steve Francis. But they needed a big man in their lineup. They needed Yao.

"We wanted this so badly, and it was very, very important," said Carroll Dawson, Rockets General Manager. "We feel very fortunate."

The Rockets sent Dawson and head coach Rudy Tomjanovich to China. They met with Yao and his parents. On June 26, 2002, it became official. The Rockets selected Yao Ming as the number one overall pick. Yao became the first-ever number one pick to come from an international basketball league. Yao's dreams had finally come true.

"This is now a new start in my basketball life," said Yao. "This is a new league, so it will be a new challenge for me. I know there will be a lot of difficulties in front of me, but I'm confident that I will learn from the NBA and improve myself and improve Chinese basketball in the future."

Everyone was excited to have Yao on the Rockets. The Rockets players and coaches couldn't wait to meet him. The Rockets were the talk of the town. There hadn't been this much excitement since the championship years.

Hundreds of fans waited for Yao at the Houston airport. Banners and welcome signs filled the terminal. Yao signed autographs and posed for pictures. The Yao Ming era in Houston officially began.

"I know I made everybody wait a long time," said Yao. "I hope everybody will think it was worth the wait."

The Center of Attention

The spotlight was bright. Everyone wanted to know: How good is Yao? Not many people in the United States had ever seen Yao play. Even NBA players wanted to know what kind of game he had. Yao felt a lot of pressure to play well.

"This is the most pressure I've ever faced in my life, but it's something I have to deal with," Yao said at the time.

Yao didn't go to training camp. He was with the Chinese National Team until the start of the NBA season. So he didn't have a lot of time to play basketball with his new teammates. He played in only two NBA preseason games. When the season started, he was

still getting used to his new city and teammates.

As a result, Yao started the season off slowly. There was a lot for him to learn.

"I don't think I have been able to show the best of my abilities yet," Yao said then. "I'm not quite used to the speed of the game, especially on offense."

But it didn't take Yao long to adjust. Yao began to move around the court with a lot more confidence. He was a force on offense and defense. During the month of December, Yao was the NBA's top rookie in the Western Conference. He led all NBA rookies in points (17.1 per game), rebounds (10.3 per game) and blocks (2.73 per game). Yao repeated the top rookie honors in February as well.

One of the highlights of the season was Yao's first game against the Los Angeles Lakers and starter Shaquille O'Neal. There was a lot of pressure on Yao to see if he could measure up against this Laker powerhouse. Yao responded by scoring 10 points, grabbing 10 rebounds, and blocking six shots. The Rockets defeated the three-time NBA champions, 108–104 in overtime.

After the game, Yao was asked what it was like playing against Shaq. "He's like a truck," Yao said through an interpreter. "I've never encountered someone that strong before. It wore me out playing him."

And what did Shaq think of the Rockets' new star?

"He's a classy guy," O'Neal said. "I was looking forward to playing him. He's a great player. It's another challange for me."

Off the court, Yao was very popular. NBA fans around the world voted for Yao to start in the 2003 NBA All-Star Game in Atlanta. Yao also started to appear in television commercials.

Yao-mania swept through the country. NBA fans from all over the United States came to Rockets games to cheer for Yao. Whether it was Detroit, New York or San Francisco, thousands of fans snapped pictures, waved signs and cheered for their new hero. This support made the 22-year-old rookie feel at home, even though he was thousands of miles away from China.

"I could feel the warmth coming from people, and it means a lot to have their support," said Yao. "I felt like I had a lot of home games, even when I was not in Houston."

It was a great season for the Rockets. Even though they missed the playoffs, the Rockets won 15 more games than they had the previous season.

Yao finished his rookie season with an average of 13.5 points, 5.8 rebounds and almost two blocks per game. He earned the Got Milk? NBA All-Rookie First Team honors. By the end of the season, Yao was not just an NBA player. He was an international superstar!

The Sky's the Limit

The future is extremely bright for Yao. He is going to have a long and successful NBA career. Yao is a good shooter and an awesome passer. Yao's presence under the basket changes an entire game. Opponents think twice about trying to score on a 7-5 center. At 23 years old, Yao is already one of the best centers in the NBA.

"With his height and competitiveness, this guy has unlimited potential to raise the bar to another level," said Hakeem Olajuwon, one of Yao's all-time favorite players.

And Yao is still getting better. Next season, everything won't be so new to him. Now he understands the game and the NBA style of play. Plus, he's had a full season to play with his new teammates. He has big plans for the future.

"My goal is for the Rockets to win a championship, and my goal for myself is to help them win a championship," said Yao.

So far, it looks like Yao definitely has what it takes. His first season, an entire country was hoping he would succeed. And he did. He never let the pressure bother him. He handles questions from reporters with a sense of humor. His lovable personality and amazing talent have won him millions of fans.

These fans have learned a lot about China by following Yao. They've learned about its customs and its people. Chinese citizens have learned a lot about Houston and the United States through Yao. This makes Yao an important international ambassador.

"Yao is so inspiring," said former Rockets coach Rudy Tomjanovich. "It just gives me goose bumps sometimes."

Yao knows there are more important things in the world than basketball. He donates his time to many good causes. In China, Yao hosted a telethon to raise money to find a cure for a disease called SARS. The telethon raised more than $300,000. A lot of Yao's NBA friends, like Shaquille O'Neal and

Magic Johnson, taped video messages asking people to help.

Yao works hard on the court, to help his team become champions. And he works hard off the court, to make the world a better place. But for Yao, all this hard work is fun. He loves being in the NBA — and his fans can tell! Everyone loves Yao, especially young fans. When asked why he is so popular with kids, Yao had a guess: "Maybe because I am a kid, too!"

READ INSIDE STUFF!

For Exclusive Behind-the-Scenes

Your

That

BA

REGULAR

ION

TING

Y FREE!

AN OFF

to NBA.com

SUBSCRIBE NOW. ©2001. SINGLE COPY PRICE $3.50.

CODE: A3CB01